Jewelry in God's Church, Why?

Charles E. Creech

All rights reserved. No part of this publication may be reproduced, distributed, or transmitted in any form or by any means, including photocopying, recording, or other electronic or mechanical methods, without the prior written permission of the publisher, except in the case of brief quotations embodied in critical reviews and certain other noncommercial uses permitted by copyright law. For permission requests, write to the publisher, TEACH Services, Inc., at the address below.

All Bible references are taken from the King James Version (KJV) of the Bible. Public domain.

HISTORICAL AND CONTEMPORARY PERSPECTIVES is a registered copyright© 1991 by Charles E. Creech. All rights reserved. No part of this book may be used or reproduced in any manner without permission except in the case of brief quotations embodied in critical articles, reviews, or lectures and credit is given accordingly.

Copyright © 2020 Charles E. Creech
Copyright © 2020 TEACH Services, Inc.
ISBN-13: 978-1-4796-1111-9 (Paperback)
ISBN-13: 978-1-4796-1112-6 (ePub)
Library of Congress Control Number: 2020912484

Published by

www.TEACHServices.com • (800) 367-1844

Dedication

For my wife, LaVern, my two children, Carla and Kevin, and in loving memory of our grand uncle, Kelly Hague—a strong advocate for maintaining Christian standards and promoting the only true Sabbath, the seventh day.

Table of Contents

Acknowledgements vi
Preface vii

Introduction. 9
Chapter 1: A Brief History of Jewelry Use. 11
Chapter 2: How Did Jewelry Get into the Church?. 18
Chapter 3: God's Attitude about Jewelry as Revealed in
          the Scriptures 24
Chapter 4: If God Didn't, Who Did? 27
Chapter 5: Abraham, Sarah, Abimelech, Pharaoh—What
          Does It All Mean? 37
Chapter 6: Church Politics and the Wedding Band 41
Chapter 7: Culture and Other Objections 44
Chapter 8: Ethical Issues Involved in Wearing the
          Wedding Band 50

Appendix A 55

Appendix B 58

Epilogue 63

Glossary 64

Bibliography 66

About the Author 68

Acknowledgements

I want to acknowledge encouragement from my former conference president of the Northeastern Conference of Seventh-day Adventists, the late George R. Earle; pastors who have used my materials; Bible instructors; and conscientious laymen who have encouraged me to make this information available to more people. Since this booklet was first published, over 6,500 copies have been circulated around the earth. While that is not a lot of copies, it does demonstrate the issue of jewelry in the Church is still alive and well and important to many Christians. Additionally, there have been requests to translate the book into French and Spanish.

My wife, LaVern, has been invaluable to me by giving me encouragement, laying out the original photocopies of the book for me, and helping me with issues of composing on the computer. My friend, Randy Hutchison, did the work on the cover of the original book. Many people across the nation have told me that such a book is much needed in today's environment of compromise among so many churchgoers and clergy alike.

This third edition is presented as a result of many readers requesting more scriptural and practical material to refer to in addressing the subject of excessive jewelry wearing and bodily adornment—especially among Christians.

Preface

The history of the book—

Jewelry in the Seventh-day Adventist Church, Why? (the first edition) evolved from a study of jewelry, which held my interest for many years ... especially after I migrated to the Northeast United States of America from the Midwest. When I needed a paper to satisfy partial requirements toward the master's degree in pastoral ministry, I utilized my research that I had been ten years in preparing.

The basic outline and principles were first presented as a sermon at my resident church in Jamaica, New York. It was a reaction to the proliferation of jewelry I saw there. The Northeastern Conference of Seventh-day Adventists president, George R. Earle, was present at the church the same day. I did not know he was coming. After hearing my sermon, he exclaimed, "Creech, I wish you would print that material and make it available to every pastor and Bible worker (teacher) in this conference!"

I told him, "I will, probably, some day." This was because I was aware that cultural differences and opinions ran very deep in the northeastern part of the United States.

As it turned out, the congregation received the sermon very positively. As a result, on the next Sabbath day, many people came and told me personally how much they appreciated the eye-opening information presented. A substantial number of them took their wedding rings off and did not put them back on.

A few months later I gave the same message at a church in the suburbs of New York City. Unbeknown to me, their nominating committee was in the clutches of an impasse concerning allowing individuals to hold high profile church offices if they wore rings. The following week I received a letter from their committee chairperson stating their profound appreciation for my giving them the information to help them make the decision to enable them to intelligently vote to implement the church's standards in reference to its elected leaders. It would be fair to state from the outset, that my findings and views are not accepted by all, depending upon what geographical and cultural background my readers have come from. This reaction is reasonably expected in these modern times. It must also be remembered, at the same time, TRUTH has always been a casualty while error flourishes unabated, openly.

In this book, *Jewelry in God's Church, Why?*, we will examine the historical evidence available, the scriptural evidence, and finally the ethical considerations and options. I hope that this work will at least inspire more serious thought, closer investigation, and deeper commitment to the timeless principles upon which the Seventh-day Adventist—and all Christian churches—are built.

Introduction

Where We Are Today ... AD 2020

The question of jewelry use among God's people has been a matter of controversy for centuries. Moses, who wrote Genesis over 1,500 years before Christ, was aware of the problem, as were many other prophets. More recently, it seems that what the Church took for granted, so to speak—that jewelry was not acceptable—has fallen into an attitude of laxness. Problems for laity and ministers alike have been compounded by the decision of the General Conference of Seventh-day Adventists to allow anyone who desires to wear a wedding band to do so "without doing violence to their conscience."

This ruling has created many hypocrites in the SDA Church. Why? Because many individuals who were married for years and wore no wedding ring and were convinced of the Biblical truthfulness of their position have now or within the past decade reverted happily to not only wearing the wedding band, but other forms of jewelry including bracelets, necklaces, other rings, earrings, nose rings, and ankle bracelets. In actuality, we see that by the Church not holding the line on the principle of modesty, they have opened the floodgates to the wearing of all forms of jewelry. Thus the former argument of cultural differences being the basis for conduct is no longer the case.

To many minds the wearing of a wedding band may or may not constitute an ethical issue. The writer believes the subject to be an ethical issue since it involves *the consideration of norms and principles, which come to bear on future consequences.*

Of late, there has been a trend to justify the wearing of some forms of jewelry based largely on the argument of cultural differences between North Americans and people groups from other countries/cultures. Again, this argument is without merit as cultures are merging today at a steady rate and there are not sharp differences existing anymore.

In this study we will take a look at the historical evidence available, the scriptural evidence, and finally the ethical considerations and options. Not only will we examine the issue of jewelry but of dress as well.

Chapter 1

A Brief History of Jewelry Use

The Ancient Uses of Jewelry as Amulets

Jewelry, by definition, is an ornament designed to adorn the person and be worn for various reasons. Their fundamental and most compelling purpose in ancient Egypt was as amulets for the protection of the wearer from mysterious and hostile forces. What were these hostile forces? Noxious animals, crocodiles, snakes, scorpions or diseases, accidents, and natural calamities such as storms or drought. To protect himself against inimical powers, the ancient primitive, like his modern counterpart (21st century humans) tied charms to his/her wrists, ankles, neck, waist, and other vulnerable points on the body.

Such talisman might consist of various stones such as carnelian, turquoise, and lapis lazuli that preserved with themselves the color of life: blood, the fresh green of spring vegetation, or the blue of water and holy sky realms.

Pebbles of the aforementioned materials had to be perforated before they could be attached by linen cords or leather thongs; thus the stone pendant was introduced and later supplemented by various shaped beads in such artificial materials as pottery, green or blue stealite, glazed quartz frit (fiaence), and glass.

"Among such magic substances must also be included gold, which was probably first found as shining granules in river sands. Gold could be worked by comparatively simple means and fashioned into gleaming beads and objects that never lost their luster but seemed to retain within themselves all the fire and glory of the sun. No wonder, therefore, that the flesh of the very gods was believed to be made of this eternally shining material."[1] Below are a view of how some of the amulets and charms looked:

The Shen of Akh, Finger Ring also Symbolic of the Sun on the Horizon

Some of the images shown here depict a few of the earliest examples of talismans, amulets, and "lucky charms" as we call them today. These images represent items from Egyptian life and religious culture of about 4,000 years BC. I will seek to identify some of them and explain their meaning and purpose, albeit their main purpose and meaning had to do with the occult, worship of their gods, and protection as they envisioned it.

---

[1] Aldred, Cyril. *Ancient Jewelry* (New York: Ballantine Books), p. 10.

A Brief History of Jewelry Use

Scarab Beetle: Millions of amulets and stamp seals of stone or faience were fashioned in Egypt depicted the scarab beetle. **Meaning**: It seemed to the ancient Egyptians that the young scarab beetles emerged spontaneously from the burrow where they were born. Therefore, they were worshipped as "Khepera," which means "he was come forth."

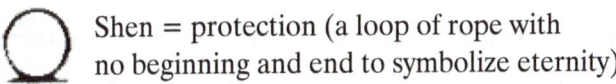

Shen = protection (a loop of rope with no beginning and end to symbolize eternity)

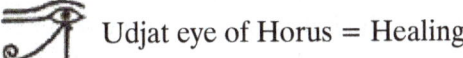

Udjat eye of Horus = Healing

Cartouche (Write your name inside the oval to protect it from harm)

Djed pillar = stability

Ankh = Life, eternal life

Sekhem = authority

While we are looking at Egyptian symbols, we should examine the **Ankh,** which is a symbol inspired by Satan to supplant the meaning and authority of the Christian cross. The fact that the ankh originated with the ancient Egyptians as a sign of perpetual life that predates Christianity and was used by Coptic Christians does in no way prove that is proper or pleases God when it is worn. The Ankh was worn as a protective talisman by both the living and the deceased.

Description: A cross shaped like a "T" with a loop at the top.

Meaning of the Ankh: To the ancient Egyptians the Ankh symbolized physical and eternal life, immortality, and reincarnation It was regarded as the key of the Nile which overflowed annually and so fertilized the land of ancient Egypt. The loop at the top of the Ankh was believed to represent the mouth of a fish which, metaphorically, flourished in the water (symbolizing the life of Egypt), bringing the inundations and renewal of the fertile soil to those who depended upon its replenishment to maintain life.

Another theory suggests that it was meant to represent the sunrise, although this is the explanation of another similar symbol called the 'Sa.' This theory suggests that the loop depicts the sun disk, the crossbar represents the line of the horizon, and the vertical bar represents the path of the sun. The 'Sa' was associated with Taweret, the ancient Egyptian hippopotamus goddess, and the dwarf god, Bes, and it symbolized the protection of young life.

The fact is that Satan understood God's promise of Genesis 3:15 and he knew that Jesus was going to die on a cross. So he simply made an attempt to pre-empt God's plan by creating a diversion—a substitute if you please—way before the Savior (Jesus) implemented it as a means of affecting the mission of Jesus in bringing salvation of the world. So, now let us talk about some of the amulets.

From the images on page 12, one can detect the very clear circle which represents the sun and thus the Sun God, Ra. The evil **Eye of Horus** is an ancient Egyptian symbol of protection, royal power, and good health. The **eye** is personified in the goddess Wadjet (also written as Wedjat, or Udjat, Uadjet, Wedjoyet, Edjo, or Uto). Wedjat "was intended to protect the pharaoh [here] in the afterlife" and to ward off evil.[2]

The Djed Pillar (page 13) was thought by the Egyptians to maintain stability.

The meaning of the **Cartouche talisman** (page 13) is found in the illustration of a magical rope which surrounded and protected the name of its wearer. The ancient Egyptians believed in magic amulets and talismans. The magical and protective power of the **Cartouche talisman** was also a charm for good wishes.

The Shen of Ahnk, pictured on page 12, is very similar to the Ahnk. A **shen** ring is a circle with a line at a tangent to it, which was represented in hieroglyphs as a stylized loop of a rope. The word **"shen"** itself means, in ancient Egyptian, "encircle," while the **shen** ring represented eternal protection. Notice the finger to the right of the Shen Ahnk amulet. It is a 100% duplicate. The purpose of the Shen of Ahnk was to provide its wearer the physical presence of the solar disk from morning to night. In other words, the Egyptians were sun worshippers.

In view of how highly the ancients regarded this precious shining metal (gold), and that most of them were worshippers of the sun, it is easy to see how they fashioned disks and rounded ornaments and eventually rings of various sizes to fit different parts of the body to keep themselves continually in contact with their gods. These golden objects allowed them the opportunity to "see" their god even when the sun was not shining.

---

[2]*The Book of the Dead,* translated by Karl Richard Lepsius, 1842. https://1ref.us/18x, accessed May 18, 2020. See also *Amulets and Superstitions*, 2nd edition, by E.A. Wallis Budge (New York: Dover Publications, 2011).

Jewels as Adornments and Aphrodisiacs

Jewels could also be used as an extension of their magic powers to enhance sexual attractiveness of the wearer in very much the same way dress and cosmetics were employed (and are still utilized today). It is when the adornment of the person becomes paramount that the artistic aspects of the jewels become as important as its amuletic significance. Thus it came to be that fillets and circlets were devised more to keep the hair in a pleasing shape than to protect the head. The artificial cowrie shells in the girdle around the waist could be filled with rattling pellets to give forth a seductive tinkle as the wearer swayed her hips in walking. Cunningly devised anklets and bracelets could enhance a slender limb or disguise a thickened joint.

> *It is when the adornment of the person becomes paramount that the artistic aspects of the jewels become as important as its amuletic significance.*

Jewelry as an Exhibition of Wealth and Status

Jewels were used to exhibit the status and wealth—and therefore the power and prestige—of the owner. There were other uses also:

1. To confer high office
2. To carry secret messages
3. To commemorate political events
4. To convey value as money
5. To carry perfume or poison

In ancient Rome, rings attained an importance they had not possessed elsewhere. *They became a part of the social system.* Hence, the admonition given in James 2:2–4:

> 2:2 "For if there come unto your assembly a man with a gold ring, in goodly apparel, and there come in also a poor man in vile raiment;

2:3 "And ye have respect to him that weareth the gay clothing, and say unto him, Sit thou here in a good place; and say to the poor, Stand thou there, or sit here under my footstool:

2:4 "Are ye not then partial in yourselves, and are become judges of evil thoughts?"

In the early days of the Roman Empire gold was scarce so rings were made mostly of iron. The wearing of gold rings was restricted to certain classes. Gold rings as a symbol of superior class distinction became meaningless toward the end of the Roman Empire because there was so much wealth anyone could wear a gold ring.

Review Questions

1. What is jewelry by definition?
2. How was jewelry originally used?
3. What made gold so attractive to people in ancient times?
4. Aside from adornment, what are the other six uses of jewelry?

Chapter 2

How Did Jewelry Get into the Church?

When people responded to the Gospel as preached by the early believers and came into the Christian church, they sought to bring their jewelry with them along with their other heathen practices. This is why the counsel of 1 Peter 3:3, 4 and 1 Timothy 2:9 is given. These admonitions precede by many years the counsel of the church fathers Cyprian and Jerome. The only kind of rings permitted to Christians were signet rings. "The early church bishop Tertullian, complained that there was too much ring wearing by Christians."[3] Church fathers Jerome and Cyprian saw a problem and cautioned against this vanity.[4] Clement of Alexandria, in a bid to stem the tide of worldliness, distinguished between the images on rings that were of pagan or immoral character and those permitted to Christians. Here can be

---
[3] De Cultu fem 1.9 (Church Fathers).
[4] De Hab. Virg. 21.

How Did Jewelry Get into the Church?

seen the "leavening process" of compromise beginning to take its toll upon the early church.

This is pointed out as happening under the symbolism of the Pergamos church, the third church of Revelation 2:14, 15. Pergamos covers the chronological period of Biblical and secular history designated as the 4th, 5th, and the first part of the 6th centuries. It was the era of state-supported religion and compromise. Legend says the Roman emperor, Constantine, and his entire army were baptized and admitted into the Catholic Church. Satan could not destroy the church by persecution, therefore he corrupted it by popularity and worldly practices. Pagan practices and beliefs then came into the church. (See Appendix B, note 1.)

> *Satan could not destroy the church by persecution, therefore he corrupted it by popularity and worldly practices.*

Around the 5th century, the Roman Empire began to be invaded by the barbarian tribes of western Europe. The Roman soldiers not only brought back the religious (pagan) philosophy (such as Mithraism) of these barbarians, but also their ornaments and practices connected with their use. The Visigoths (early Germans) and Lombards (Germans who migrated to Italy) are credited with giving Rome the betrothal ring. So, where did Rome get the practice from? *Directly from the pagans!* The historian, Gregory of Tours, mentions the widespread use of the betrothal ring by these barbarian tribes.[5]

By the 7th century the church had begun to use the ring as a symbol of investiture. The following quotes illustrate that even in the administration of the wedding vow with the use of rings, the custom is pagan. "The custom of placing the betrothal or wedding ring upon the fourth finger seems undoubtedly to trace its origin to the fancy that a special nerve or vein runs directly from this finger to the heart. Macrobius, in his *Saturnalia*, alludes to the belief in the following words: 'Because of this nerve, the newly betrothed

---
[5]Gregory of Tours, *Vitae Patrum* 20, Chapter 17: "Marrying in the Frankish Church, The Nuptial Process."

places the ring on this finger of his spouse, as though it was a representation of the heart."[6] Macrobius asserts that he derived his information from an Egyptian priest. Naturally this is of pagan origin. (See Appendix B, note 2.)

It has been conjectured that this was not the source of the custom, but that in the church service it was usual for the Christian priest to touch three fingers successively with the ring while saying: "In the name of the Father, of the Son and of the Holy Ghost," and then to place it upon the last finger touched. We do know that this was the usage in the bestowal of Episcopal rings and later with wedding rings, but the excerpted statement cited from the pagan writer Macrobius states that "in earlier marriage or betrothal ceremony the custom must have had an entirely different origin."[7] (See Appendix A, note 1.)

Taking a look at other sources, we notice that "Neither the Bible nor the Talmud speaks of the ring as symbolic of marriage."[8] *The Jewish Encyclopedia* credits the Romans with the influence exerted which led to the use of rings in weddings. For them, only one ring was to be given and by the bridegroom only. This source also states that "Jewish women *were not in a habit of wearing their wedding rings* which were sometimes larger or very small. The rings served occasionally as bouquet holders, the myrtle branches being inserted in them at weddings."[9]

As late as the 16th century, Jewish women were not to wear weddings rings. In fact, Jewish people at large were discouraged from wearing any ornaments at all. Although women of the Christian church were taught to avoid all superfluous adornments, the wearing of a gold ring was permitted to them. This was not, however, to be considered as an ornament, but simply for use in sealing up the household goods entrusted to a wife's care. Nevertheless, while noting this use, Clemens Alexandrinus

---

[6]Macrobius, *Saturnalia,* lib. vii, cap. 13.
[7]Newman, Cardinal J.H. *Development of Christian Doctrine, an Essay* (London: Longmans, Green, and Co., 1909), pp. 272, 273.
[8]Kunz, George F. *The Jewish Encyclopedia,* "Rings for the Finger" (New York: Funk and Wagnalls, 1906), p. 430.
[9]Lecky, W.E.H. "Rationalism in Europe," qtd. in *The Jewish Encyclopedia* (New York: Funk and Wagnalls, 1906).

(ca AD 150–217) adds that, "If both servants and masters were properly instructed in their respective duties and obligations, there would be no need for such precautions."[10]

Coming back to the 16th century, one can perceive that by then although church leaders had voiced their opposition to jewelry and especially rings, ornaments were deeply entrenched. It appears that an accommodation similar to that of allowing divorce was yielded to in the case of the wedding ring. It was not wanted. It was wrong, but suffered nevertheless because of the strong will of the people.

"In Poland where the Christian inhabitants laid great stress on the wearing of rings, it was not until the reign of Sigismund Augustus (1506–1548) that the Jews, after long debates in Reichstag, were allowed to wear such ornaments. These had to be inscribed with the words 'Sabbath' or 'Jerusalem' which according to Leiwel, was intended to remind Jews of the wrath of God and of the punishment of their sins."[11]

"At a later period rings bearing the name of God were used as amulets [definitely pagan in origin]. When a fondness for ring wearing became too pronounced, the rabbis or congregation interfered. Thus for example, the rabbinical convention at Bologna in 1416 AD decreed that no man might wear more than one and no woman more than three rings."[12] Along this same line, the Frankfort sumptuary regulation of 1715 enacted that "Young girls may wear no rings whatever."[13]

All of the foregoing illustrate the fact that the use of rings in the church for whatever reason and by whoever was forbidden and evolved strictly as a human invention adapted from the pagan world. The Catholic and Jewish churches both fought against the practice, but, as in many other areas, could not

---

[10]Clementis Alenandrini, Pedagogus. qtd. in Kunz, "Rings for the Finger," *The Jewish Encyclopedia* (New York: Funk and Wagnalls, 1906).
[11]Gesch, Sternbert. *Der Juden in Polen*, p. 146. *The Jewish Encyclopedia*, vol. 10 (New York: Funk and Wagnalls, 1906), p. 430.
[12]Vogelstein and Rieger, qtd. in *The Jewish Encyclopedia* (New York: Funk and Wagnalls, 1906), p. 337.
[13]Judische Meichwurdigkeiten, Schudt IV 3,99, qtd. in *The Jewish Encyclopedia*, vol. 10 (New York: Funk and Wagnalls, 1906), p. 430.

stem the tide of tradition and paganism which had successfully invaded the church. Church leaders were powerless to keep it out. Instead, they devised ways in which the rings could become legal and acceptable by the church. The writer observes, however, that this attitude manifested by the church is very similar to the attitudes of:

1. Cain bringing fruit instead of flesh, and expecting God's blessing (Gen. 4:3–5).
2. The two young men, Nadab and Abihu, who offered "strange fire" before God and expected Him to accept it (Num. 3:4).
3. The Roman Catholic Church, who tried to transfer the solemnity of the seventh day Sabbath to Sunday.

> *What God has not put His blessing upon, we have no authority to make "holy" or acceptable through civil law, religious law, traditional use, or cultural use.*

In any case, what God has not put His blessing upon, we have no authority to make "holy" or acceptable through civil law, religious law, traditional use, or cultural use. Jesus was concerned about the tendency of people to "seek to change the rules" while at the same time professing to be righteous (Matt. 15:9). We are now ready to examine the biblical evidences—explicit or implicit—which touch on the subject of jewelry.

Review Questions

1. What counsel did Peter give concerning rings? (1 Peter 3:3, 4)
2. What did Paul write to Timothy about jewelry? (1 Tim.2:9)
3. What happened to the church during the 4th to the 6th centuries?
4. In addition to the church suffering from internal compromise and corruption, what other forces caused problems?
5. What is the origin of using rings in weddings?

6. How did the church quiet her conscience in the matter of ring-wearing?
7. What attitude did the Catholic or early Christian church take toward the wedding ring practice?
8. Why did the church allow rings and jewelry to be worn by its adherents?
9. Give three examples of what attempting to make rings and other jewelry acceptable to God approximates in principle.
10. How did the Jewish leaders in the 16th century feel about wearing wedding rings?
11. What ruse was invented to allow the common Christian people in Western Europe to wear rings?
12. What attitude should true Christians take toward unbiblical or pagan practices allowed by churches?

Chapter 3

God's Attitude about Jewelry as Revealed in the Scriptures

The first thing we need to establish is that God does not have a negative attitude about jewels. George Vandeman, in his book *God Loves Jewelry*, makes this point very clear. The problem is that human nature, being what it is because of sin, does not allow the majority of us to wear jewels without "showing off." In most cases, we at least feel somewhat proud. The inspired Christian writer, Mrs. Ellen G. White, comments on 1 Timothy 2:9: "Here the Lord, through his apostle, speaks expressly against the wearing of gold. Let those who have had experience see to it that they do not lead others astray on this point by their example. That ring encircling your finger may be very plain, but it is useless, and the wearing of it has a wrong influence upon others."[14] *The Seventh-Day Adventist Church Manual* states on pages 145 and 146

---

[14]White, *Testimonies for the Church,* Vol. 4 (Mountain View, CA: Pacific Press Publishing Association, 1881), p. 630.

that: "The wearing of ornaments of jewelry is a bid for attention which is not in keeping with Christ self-forgetfulness." With that said, let us move on.

When we think of controversial subjects in the church, we could argue back and forth until Jesus comes. There has always been controversy since the entrance of sin. Therefore, there must be some standard to which we can refer to test our positions. We must ask some very crucial questions, such as: Do God's rules govern His church? Or do our own rules govern the church? And regarding the rules that God has made—are they a bunch of unnecessary prohibitions or are they dependable regulations given in love to help keep us happy so we can enjoy a relationship with Him better? It is sad to say; but some of us are so set in our own opinions that one wonders if a true biblical position was presented by an angel from heaven, would it be accepted any

> *There has always been controversy since the entrance of sin. Therefore, there must be some standard to which we can refer to test our positions.*

more readily? Someone has suggested that our relationship with God, once we have become Christians, is similar to that of marriage. Marriage *is* a very restrictive arrangement—but with very beneficial results. However, a new bride or groom are not often seen or heard complaining about apparent restrictions if *they truly love each other!*

It is only "if something happens" and they don't love each other anymore that they become unhappy, fault-finding, long faced, and miserable. Marriage partners are happiest when both parties are exerting all or most of their effort at making each other happy. *They do not need a long list of "dos and don'ts"* because their focus is to please each other and not solely themselves.

As in marriage, the attitude of the Christian is one of love based on a consuming desire to please the Savior. We are married to Christ and as such we want to please Him. On the other hand, Christians who do not love Jesus could be characterized as being long faced and miserable, constantly looking for an opportunity to please themselves which ultimately leads to compromise.

Since we have discussed elsewhere in this treatise where jewelry started and how it got into the church, we now want to consider this: What does the Bible tell us about the wedding ring or the lack of it?

Review Questions

1. Does God have a negative attitude in regard to jewels?
2. If God does not have a problem with jewels, then what is the problem with people wearing them?
3. What principle should govern what a Christian does or does not do?

Chapter 4

If God Didn't, Who Did?

The background to this approach is found in the human experience. Simply stated: "When there's a problem, solve it!" The greatest achievements known to civilization have risen out of a need to remedy some difficult situation, to simplify some process or to prevent some unfavorable eventuality. To illustrate this point, let us look at three incidents recorded in the book of Genesis.

A problem existed in each example below, but what was the solution? Let us discover what, if any, remedy was prescribed by God for the problem which existed.

1. Genesis 12:10–20 gives the account of Abraham, Sarah, and Pharaoh. Abraham and Sarah were traveling through Egypt. Sarah was very beautiful as previously noted and because Abraham was afraid the Egyptians would kill him for his wife, he decided to lie and told Pharoah that Sarah was his sister.

2. Genesis 20:1–18 records the story of Abraham and Sarah as they traveled through Gerar. Sarah was a very beautiful woman and Abraham was worried that harm would befall him if he were discovered to be her husband. Therefore, Abraham contrived a lie, telling King Abimelech that Sarah, his wife, was "my sister." The contextual reading reveals that King Abimelech was given a dream that told him Sarah's true status. With a threat of immediate death, unless he complied, Abimelech was commanded by God to restore to Abraham his wife. Also, because of Sarah, God had prevented the women in Abimelech's house (perhaps a harem) from conceiving children. When Sarah was released, their wombs were again made fertile. The *married couple* was sent on their way with many gifts from an apologetic Abimelech.
3. Genesis 26:6–11 relates the story of Isaac and Rebekah who encountered another King Abimelech in Gerar. Isaac fell into the same trap as his father. He also lied to protect his life since in his mind he was sure he would be killed by the men of Gerar who would then take his beautiful wife for themselves. Isaac and Rebekah lived in Gerar under an incognito guise of "sister and brother" for a long time. It just so happened that one day Abimelech looked out of his window and observed Isaac and Rebekah "sporting." In our vernacular today, we might say "fooling around." He perceived that their relationship with each other was something other than a sibling relationship. It dawned upon him: "THEY MUST BE MAN AND WIFE!"

Abimelech may have had moral problems by our standard, but apparently he did not wish to add wife-stealing to the list. He quickly summoned Isaac to his court, rebuked him sharply for lying to him, which had jeopardized his welfare, and commanded all of his people not so much as to touch this couple! One can imagine Abimelech letting out a sigh of relief as those liars disappeared over the horizon, leaving his house in peace.

As a result of being deceived, Pharaoh took Sarah into his house with a clear conscience. But then the monarch's house was plagued with "great plagues." The Bible does not reveal how Pharaoh was made aware, but he did discover that Abraham and Sarah were lying about their marital status and that they were indeed married. He called Abraham before him and berated him for lying to him. Because of this incident, Pharaoh was very indignant and sent the couple away with the gifts he had given to Sarah.

Many individuals who want to wear jewelry try to say the Bible makes a weak case against the practice. However, nothing could be further from the truth!

Many individuals who want to wear jewelry try to say the Bible makes a weak case against the practice. However, nothing could be further from the truth! A careful, unbiased reading of Genesis 35:1–4 makes this clear:

> 35:1 And God said unto Jacob, Arise, go up to Bethel, and dwell there: and make there an altar unto God, that appeared unto thee when thou fleddest from the face of Esau thy brother.
>
> 35:2 Then Jacob said unto his household, and to all that were with him, Put away the strange gods that are among you, and be clean, and change your garments.
>
> 35:3 And let us arise, and go up to Bethel; and I will make there an altar unto God, who answered me in the day of my distress, and was with me in the way which I went.
>
> 35:4 And they gave unto Jacob all the strange gods which were in their hand, and all their earrings which were in their ears; and Jacob hid them under the oak which was by Shechem.

The foregoing text reminds us that God's people had adopted the heathen and amuletic practices of the tribes that surrounded them. It tells us that the "strange gods in their hands" were the images of the local false deities. Additionally, Jacob's people were to hand over "all their earrings which were in their ears" as they were wearing the earrings in opposition to God's will.

Normally if any person will wear earrings, he or she will have no reservations about wearing other forms of jewelry, including the finger ring. The important thing is, that God, in His instructions to Jacob, lumped them all into one category. He said "Get rid of the foreign gods you have with you, and purify yourselves and change your clothes" (paraphrased).

There is a strong implication that God did not want them to appear before Him in the trappings of another god. The basis for His reaction can be best described in His own words: "Thou shalt have no other gods before me ... I am a jealous God."[15] It may be characterized as a husband seeing his wife wearing clothes or ornaments given to her by her illicit lover and flaunting them "in his face," so to speak. This is repugnant! It is adultery—spiritual adultery. That is why God was always referring to Israel as a whore.

Does the Bible Teach that it is Acceptable for Men to Wear Earrings?

Judges 8:24 indicates that the heathen enemies of Israel wore gold earrings. The fact is that the soldiers of Israel did not, and in the heat of battle it was indeed not safe for them to be found in golden earrings. It was like a kind of sign or uniform inasmuch as they looked a lot alike racially and physically. Soldiers with earrings were killed on the spot, no questions asked! Shall we have a discussion about men wearing earrings at this point? Yes! Let's go!

Well, let us consult the Word to see what He reveals to us. We see so many men and boys wearing earrings nowadays, some of us wonder if there is anything in the Bible about this pro or con.

Abraham's son, Isaac, needed a wife, but not just any woman. This had to be a woman who believed in the true God like

---

[15]Exod. 20:3, 5. Also see Judges 8:24: "And Gideon said unto them, I would desire a request of you, that ye would give me every man the earrings of his prey. (For they had golden earrings, because they were Ishmaelites.)"

If God Didn't, Who Did?

Abraham's family and near kin. Isaac was special since he was the miracle child of promise through whose lineage the Messiah would come. God directed Abraham to send a servant to another geographical area to find the right girl for his son. Her name was Rebekah. The following verses tell the story. In Genesis 24:16–22, and 47, we read:

> 24:16 And the damsel was very fair to look upon, a virgin, neither had any man known her: and she went down to the well, and filled her pitcher, and came up.

> 24:17 And the servant ran to meet her, and said, Let me, I pray thee, drink a little water of thy pitcher.

> 24:18 And she said, Drink, my lord: and she hasted, and let down her pitcher upon her hand, and gave him drink.

> 24:19 And when she had done giving him drink, she said, I will draw water for thy camels also, until they have done drinking.

24:20 And she hasted, and emptied her pitcher into the trough, and ran again unto the well to draw water, and drew for all his camels.

24:21 And the man wondering at her held his peace, to wit whether the Lord had made his journey prosperous or not.

24:22 And it came to pass, as the camels had done drinking, that the man took a golden earring of half a shekel weight, and two bracelets for her hands of ten shekels weight of gold ...

24:47 And I asked her, and said, Whose daughter art thou? And she said, the daughter of Bethuel, Nahor's son, whom Milcah bare unto him: and I put the earring upon her face, and the bracelets upon her hands.

Verse 47 states that Abraham's servant, Eliezer, put the earring *upon her face.* The practice was actually a Bedouin custom used to this day to indicate betrothal or engagement. It was in reality a nose ring—not two earrings. Many advocates of adornment erroneously use this Biblical account to justify the wearing of jewelry. We will address this later.

Earrings have, over the centuries, been a sign of a myriad of things such as prostitution, wealth, nobility, slavery, keeping out demons, fertility, and probably many other situations and conditions. Jillian Downer, in *Our Everyday Life,* September 28, 2017, presents that the tradition of men wearing earrings is also connected to primitive Indian tribes who used facial piercings and jewelry as tools to modify their bodies for religious and cultural initiation and rituals.

Still used in these cultures today, body modification is often a symbol of age, status, wealth, and standing within the tribe. In the 1920s, it became popular for sailors to pierce their ears based on superstition. It was believed that if their bodies were recovered at sea the person finding them could take the earring as payment for a proper burial. Sailors who had sailed around the world or survived a sinking ship also had earrings to document their experiences. Thus, the phenomena of men with earrings may still seem strange to some, but they have been worn by men since the beginning of time.

So, in these current days, why would men wear earrings? Abeer Jain, a gemstone manufacturer, offers ten specific reasons why men wear them:

1. **A Fashion Trend.** Young men find this to be an enhancement to their looks, and wearing earrings, therefore, is a definite fashion statement.
2. **A Religious Custom or Tradition.** In some religions such as Hindu, ear piercing for both sexes is conducted in the 4th or 5th year of life and celebrated by a major feast with relatives and friends.
3. **To Rebel.** Jain makes another important point when he states another reason men wear earrings is that they are attempting to rebel against something. It could be rebelling against society, parents, or just to be different and stand out in a crowd.
4. **As a Symbol of Status or Wealth.** Some guys wear diamond studs that broadcast their wealth. Some will even use the diamond as a savings for hard times and use the proceeds of their adornment in the event they fall on hard times.
5. **Actors in Character.** Some men are playing a role in a movie or play that requires them to have a piercing on one or both sides to fall into character.
6. **To Look "Cool" and be Attractive to Women.** Some men feel that women are attracted to men that wear earrings and it makes them feel as they are more apt to attract the opposite sex.
7. **A Gift.** Often a man may have received a gift from a friend, wife, or girlfriend that causes him to get a piercing of one or both ears.
8. **Presenting your Sexuality or Making a Statement.** There are many reasons to wear earrings as a statement. Sometimes criminals use this as a signaling process for their various capers or in pick-pocketing activities. Though disputed by some, historically the wearing of a single earring or stud on the right ear

is considered a sign of homosexuality. In today's society, however, it is common to find heterosexual men wearing earrings in both ears at once, as well as either their left or right alone and it is considered old-fashioned to wear a single earring as a sexual signal.

9. **Therapeutic Benefit.** A closely held view among pirates was that their long-distance vision was better with earrings. Although disputed these days, the lobule is an acupuncture site for vision but it is not used among acupuncture professionals for increasing vision, but more for drug dependency, eating disorders, etc. Others also believe that the wearing of gold or other precious metal in this area transfers some of the metal's properties to the person, thus offering a therapeutic benefit.

10. **Spirituality.** In some religions, such as Buddhism, the piercing of the earlobe and stretching of the opening is considered a sign of spiritual development and spiritual development. The bigger the opening the greater the spiritual development.

In Exodus 33:1–6, God was deeply concerned about the spiritual declension and amalgamation with the surrounding heathen nations while they were on their way to the Promised Land. God commanded them to take off their ornaments so He could relate to them properly. Obviously their attitude about Him and these "ornament gods" stood in the way of unimpeded communication. The Bible says they stripped off their jewelry. Now it would seem logical that if the ornaments were not acceptable to be in God's presence when they came to Him in corporate worship or convocation, why do we want to wear them in church? And since we are supposed to be in God presence always, why would we want to wear them at all at other times? Does God put on a blind or do we assume He is blind and cannot see what we are doing? Jeremiah 4:30 depicts one who is bedecked with jewelry and paints as "devastated."

Ezekiel 23:40 describes the undesirable state of God's people in unflattering terms that are usually reserved for prostitutes. Since God looks so unfavorably upon such a display, why should

If God Didn't, Who Did?

Bible-believing Christians look for ways to make it acceptable? Is there something wrong with God's standards that we humans must correct?

Many Christians are familiar with the denunciations of outward adornment recorded in Isaiah 3:16–26. While the writer of this text was denouncing the spiritual condition of the nation of Israel, the lesson is not lost on individuals who are equally as decadent. The prophet does not leave anything off his list of ornaments.

As previously stated, Rebekah was given an earring and bracelets for her hands by Abraham's servant when he found her (Gen. 24:15–27). This story seems contradictory to a Bible believer who accepts that jewelry is used for adornment in most cases. Subsequently, one could immediately jump to the conclusion that God approved of jewelry being worn on the body and that it was appropriate. *Is there an explanation for this?*

Yes, please keep in mind that God's chosen people always lived in the land of, and "rubbed shoulders" with, the idolaters, heathen worshippers, immorality, homosexuality, etc. We saw earlier even Jacob lived in Shalem and God gave him a directive to go to Bethel and make an altar and worship Him. Apparently, this action was very much needed to get him and his household back on track. Genesis 35:1–4 tells us that because of their lifestyle, adopted from the local culture, they had to divest themselves of all of their gods before they came into God's presence to worship Him. Therefore, they gave Jacob all their "strange gods" which were in their hand (finger rings, bracelets, etc.) and strange gods in their ears (earrings) and Jacob hid them under the oak which was by Shechem.

Getting back to the issue of Abraham sending Rebekah jewelry, we can still see that jewelry represented a store of value to be easily and safely transported (on the body). Therefore, we can reasonably conclude that the bracelets and earring received by Rebekah essentially represented nearly five to six ounces of gold or a monetary value of $7,800.00 in 2019 (about $159.00 in Abraham's day). Abraham's gift carried to Rebekah by Eliezer simply represented an effort to impress her father that Isaac would be able to provide for her material needs. This story does not legitimize the wearing of nose rings, earrings or bracelets.

The question we are considering is: "IF GOD DIDN'T, WHO DID?" Obviously and unequivocally God did not authorize the use of jewelry as human adornment.

Review Questions

1. Three accounts are given in Genesis wherein a means of physically announcing one's marital status would have been ideal. How could a piece of jewelry or other sign have helped the situation?
2. Would you have suggested a wedding ring?

Chapter 5

Abraham, Sarah, Abimelech, Pharaoh—What Does It All Mean?

Maybe this was God's way for them to collect items they needed for their home. Maybe Hebrews were generally mistreated in those days. Neither of these explanations make much sense, for God is able to supply all of our needs without resorting to such subterfuge.

In light of our overall discussion, the first point stands out in stark reality: Abraham, Sarah, Isaac, and Rebekah all flunked their "ethics test." Secondly, they failed because *they were expected to tell the truth.* There is evidence that these kings, though not worshippers of the true God, nevertheless knew about the God of the "Habiru" (later known as the Hebrews). There was no reason for Abraham and Isaac to lie for God was able to honor their faith and deliver them (Dan. 3:18). In each of the cited incidents, one common requirement pervades: GOD EXPECTED ABRAHAM AND ISAAC TO TELL THE TRUTH ABOUT THEIR MARITAL STATUS!

Why did they feel they had to lie? The answer is simply this: they did not have enough faith in God that He could take care of them even among those mean, unscrupulous men of Gerar and Egypt. As a result of these strong-men-of-faith-turned-weakling misrepresenting their marital status, two kings were discomfited almost to the point of death ... one king possibly jeopardized twice.

One would think that if ever a situation existed wherein a universally accepted and recognized sign of marital status was needed, this was certainly the time and place! However, no matter what precedent we look for there is none to be found here or anywhere in the Bible. Was God any less innovative than human beings are? Why did He not "come up with" such a good idea as man has invented for the use of the (forbidden symbol) ring?

This writer believes as others, such as Ellen G. White, that God wanted people then as now to confess with their mouth and demonstrate by their lifestyle the integrity of their marital status. "We need not wear the sign, for we are not untrue to our marriage vow, and the wearing of the ring would be no evidence that we are true. I feel deeply over this leavening process which seems to be going on among us, in the conformity to custom and fashion."[16]

So then, we conclude that since God did not institute the wearing of a wedding ring, IT IS APPARENTLY AN INVENTION OF MAN. My question to you dear reader is, "Are you comfortable putting your faith and trust in the traditions and inventions of men?" Many individuals who want to wear jewelry try to say the Bible makes a weak case against the practice. However, nothing could be further from the truth! A careful and unbiased reading of Genesis 35:1–4 tells us that the

---

[16]White, *Testimonies to Minister and Gospel Workers* (Mountain View, CA: Pacific Press Publishing Association, 1923), pp. 180, 181.

"strange gods in their hands" were the images of the local false deities. Jacob's people wore earrings.

Conclusions

Surely the foregoing is a clear indication of God's negative attitude concerning Israel's apostasy and adoption of heathen practices in evidence all around them. Further, one must find it very difficult to overlook the clearly negative attitude God has pertaining to the outward appearance of persons attired as described in Isaiah 3:16–26. The question we are considering is: "IF GOD DIDN'T, WHO DID?" As previously mentioned, obviously and unequivocally God did not authorize the use of jewelry as human adornment.

Some argue the point that "the ring used to be pagan, but now it is not pagan." The folly of such reasoning is illustrated by a lesson in contrast. Judges 8:24–27 gives the account of Gideon when he took the gold from the earrings of the heathen dead soldiers and made an ephod with them (an ephod is an upper garment worn by a Jewish high priest). He and his followers worshipped the ephod. Consequently, the ephod became a great source of trouble for them. Although God had blessed him in the past, "his sin consisted in taking over the prerogatives of the Aaronic priesthood without divine sanction."[17]

Additionally, Gideon's problem was that he was trying to make something holy which God had not made holy. It is not that the symbol was not holy—it was—but Gideon did not have the authority to use it. God in His sovereignty could and may command jewelry to be brought and transformed into instruments to be used in worship, but we mortals do not have that prerogative. WE CANNOT TAKE THE PAGAN-RING-TURNED-WEDDING RING AND CLEAN IT UP TO MAKE IT A HOLY SYMBOL NO MATTER WHAT WE DO. (Appendix A, note 1)

Review Questions

(Circle and answer)

1. True or False: God expected Abraham and Isaac to tell the truth about their marital status.
2. True or False: The wedding ring is an invention of man and tradition.
3. True or False: The wedding ring is pagan in origin.
4. True or False: Trying to make the wedding ring holy is like trying to make Sunday the Sabbath.

---

[17]*The Seventh-Day Adventist Bible Commentary*, Vol. 2 (Washington, DC: Review and Herald Publishing Association, 1953), pp. 354, 355.

Chapter 6

Church Politics and the Wedding Band

Some youth today are exploiting a situation created inadvertently by the General Conference of Seventh-day Adventists to accommodate members of the "Third World countries." When the SDA church began many years ago in Northern New England, it was coming from a strong Puritan background. One should remember that the Christians who had left the Anglican Church in England to come to America were doing so to rid themselves of many of the "pollutions of Rome."[18] This helps to explain why the church for many years was led and guided by strong resistance to worldly practices and customs. In the 1870s when missionary outreach went forward, these strong spiritual values were exported as well. Consequently, when they went into an area and the local culture allowed a man to have five wives, he was told

---
[18]McCarthy, James R. "Pollutions of Rome," in *Rings Through the Ages* (New York: Harper & Brothers, 1945), p. 2.

four would have to be discarded. Whatever was in opposition to the Gospel had to be put aside in those days, including the wedding ring, which was in the more advanced societies. (Appendix A, note 2)

Europeans and European-dominated societies found in South America, parts of Africa, and the tropical islands have been steeped in Catholic tradition since the times of Constantine. We have already shown how jewelry came into the church generally elsewhere in this treatise. Nothing changed with the Catholics as time progressed; but rather became more entrenched and immortalized through tradition.

When Europeans began to colonize, they brought their culture, traditions, religions, and civil laws with them. By taking a look at the various European mother countries, it is easy to see how well imprinted the respective colonies are. For many years the world SDA church was dominated by North American values because North America was in the majority demographically and financially. In political jargon, they were able "to call the shots." However, in the last thirty years or five General Conference sessions, the third world church and Americans are no longer able to hold the line against these waves of assaults which are "leavening" the pure principles once held in high esteem. The General Conference of Seventh-day Adventists, by permitting comprise through permissiveness and an inappropriate desire to please every culture group regardless of principle, has allowed the standards to be weakened. This attitude has created a climate conducive to rebellion—especially here in the United States. As stated earlier, the youth in our colleges, the unconverted in our churches are exploiting the mistake made by the General Conference with great success. They ask the brutally logical question: "WHAT'S THE DIFFERENCE IN RINGS? A ring is jewelry. How can you now tell me that I cannot wear earrings or a nose jewel or anything else?" And they are correct! Ministers, school administrators, teachers, and Bible workers cannot explain with reliable credibility how a wedding ring can be okay but other jewelry is not acceptable. This is the main reason our churches and school campuses are exhibiting an explosion of jewelry never seen heretofore. Even the "leading men" at the top are affected by this worldly custom. They allow their wives and sometimes even they wear rings. Can we realistically expect these men to erect a standard against what they have been trained by tradition and lifestyle to believe is right and proper? Dissenting voices calling for reform will have to come from elsewhere because the General Conference appears to be impotent as far as some church standards are concerned.

Now we will take a detailed look at the so-called culture issue which many ring wearers lean on so heavily.

Review Questions

1. What roles have politics and demographics played in the growth of jewelry in general and the wedding ring in particular in the SDA Church?
2. How has the permission allowed by the Church for the wedding ring led to proliferation of all other forms of jewelry among Christians?

Chapter 7

Culture and Other Objections

People need to "wake up and smell the Postum®" (coffee) as it were. *The wedding ring is a religious issue!* It has always been a religious issue since its introduction into Western society. It *became* a cultural issue as it became intertwined with religious experience and religious tradition and worked its way into everyday life and eventually into "defacto civil law." The ring is at present a religious and *ethical* issue that is perceived as a cultural issue. Perception is not reality.

Many have sought to argue away the fact that the wedding band is unacceptable for the SDA Christian on the basis of culture. They complain, "North Americans are trying to make us change our culture. This is not our culture! That is their culture!"

The reasoning that culture overrules the standard set for God's chosen people is faulty. God has been waging war against "culture" since humans left the Garden of Eden. Culture, unless it is derived from God, is an unacceptable man-made invention. However, we must admit, that God suffers it and tries to work within it to accomplish His ends. A case in point is divorce. The preponderance of Biblical evidence reveals a God who is trying to get us to do away with all of our polluted "culture" and take on that lifestyle which is genuine.

While many customs and practices have lofty goals and high ideals, they are usually hopelessly interwoven with false culture characterized by false worship, superstition, idolatry, selfishness, and many other negative values. GOD'S IDEAL FOR HIS CHOSEN PEOPLE TRANSCENDS EVERYTHING ... INCLUDING CULTURE. In the final analysis culture is not a safe guide because Satan has polluted the "ways of man" over the millenniums of human history. The writer is aware that all of the possible objections cannot be addressed within the scope of this book. Even if it were possible, there would be those who would endeavor to "spiritualize away" the evidence by saying it makes no difference as long as you love your fellow man, etc. Nevertheless, we will look at a few of the prominent excuses advanced to support the wearing of the wedding band.

Excuses Offered for Wearing Rings

1. "Americans don't like us and our culture."

    Some people from the areas where rings are worn often mix up the issues and try to say that Americans are attacking them personally and trying to change them and their culture. This is not the case however because there are many honest, enlightened, and uncompromising people in these same cultures who recognize that the wedding ring is at best not necessary and at worst is a farce that allows people to indulge their desire to adorn themselves with jewelry.

    Older Adventists from these same areas state that in the early years (the 20s to the 50s) they did not wear wedding rings. This was told to the writer in 1978. No doubt some of these people are dead by now, for they were elderly Adventists even then. I might add here, that the fact that at this writing in 2020, the principle of modesty is still alive and well and incumbent upon all Christians to observe.

2. "Isn't a tie pin, a brooch, and a watch jewelry?"

Yes, they are jewelry. Is a tie pen, brooch, or watch necessary to order, safety, or cleanliness? A tie pen keeps a man's tie from falling into his plate while eating. When brushing the teeth or performing other duties over or near messy situations at chest level, the tie pin is indispensable. If one is not needed, do not use one. If one is needed, make it as modest as possible—the smaller and less noticeable, the better. Now the brooch is another matter. Since they are worn on the clothing, their role is almost always embellishment and ornamentation. This may be difficult for some women, but they should find ways to dress up their outfits without the use of this form of ornamentation. And the watch ... watches are indispensable in this day and age. Our lives would be chaos without a durable and dependable timepiece. The watch should be of good quality so it will serve for a long time. The metal should not be so cheap that it will irritate or inflame the skin. On the other hand, if it is too flashy, or embellished too much, too big, etc., people will know that we have passed the point of utility and have entered into vanity. You will know that if you get a large number of compliments on the beauty of your watch, it is much closer to being jewelry and not just a timepiece.

3. Some cultures reject the wearing of clerical robes as being of Catholic origin and ask the question: "Why do you wear it?"

In the first place, the wearing of robes and vestments did not come from the Catholics. The Catholics copied their tradition from the Bible ... from the Aaronic priesthood and the Sanctuary system. There is nothing wrong with a minister wearing a robe into the pulpit.

4. When a jewelry-wearer is approached, you will likely hear, "What I do is my own business, I am not bothering anyone

but myself." "Don't judge me!" —a common defense of many individuals in the 21st century.

> *Do not fool yourself into thinking your influence does not count. It does.*

This is an extremely callous if not grossly uninformed position to take. The Bible and Spirit of Prophecy are replete with counsel concerning the influence we may exert on others for good or evil. Do not fool yourself into thinking your influence does not count. It does.

5. "My husband says I must wear my ring or he will leave me."

If you have this problem, you are in real trouble. Your husband apparently does not love or trust you very much if he will divorce you about something so trivial as not wearing his ring.

If this is the only guarantee that he has against your potential infidelity, he is in bad shape. His bond to you must be very weak if he cannot trust you to, by your conduct and speech, indicate to would-be "other lovers" that you are already taken and wish no further involvement with anyone other than your husband. That is really what your husband wants you to say and demonstrate. That is what will make him feel safe, secure, proud, and loved. Without this kind of loving, trusting relationship, the wedding ring takes on the character of nothing more than a cattle brand or a sign of chattel put on a slave to show ownership. (Appendix A, note 4)

Think about it, dear Reader. Maybe you need to work on your marriage relationship with your spouse. You are not simply property; and if you are being true to your marriage vow, why should you be treated with suspicion just because you decide not to wear the ring in response to obeying the will of God?

6. "The ring stops people from flirting because they always know you are married."

Nonsense! Everyone knows that the ring stops no one from "making passes" nowadays. When people really want to get into a serious extramarital affair, they take the ring off. Sometimes they leave it on and they and the other person simply ignore it. In other words, very few extramarital affairs are carried on without the parties knowing the marital status of each other. They know; but their inordinate affections rule out principle.

7. "I feel bad being pregnant without a ring on my finger so that people know I am married. When I go to the hospital for delivery, I might be shunned."

There is something wrong with society when they assume that a pregnant woman is carrying an illegitimate child simply because she does not have a ring on. On the contrary, the woman should be assumed married until proven otherwise. The problem is not with the pregnant woman. The problem is

Culture and Other Objections

with the sad state of morality in society. If one has the proper insurance coverage, married or single, the hospital is obligated to take the patient.

9. "What about the parable of the prodigal son?"

The parable of the prodigal son in Luke 15:11–32 is simply a teaching device which Jesus and others used with great facility in those days. We call them "illustrations" today. We still, in these modern days, take something from that which is familiar to us to explain a matter that is obscure, new, or difficult for us to understand. As we look closely at this parable, there are a couple points that stand out:

A. The subject of Jesus' discourse was not rings. He was not advocating the use of rings. He was teaching the value of forgiveness and the intensity of a father's love. No doubt the incident had taken place in real life for Christ did not deal in the purely abstract in His teaching methods.
B. If we are to take this parable as Jesus advocating the wearing of rings, we are missing the point. First, we need to understand that the ring put upon the finger of the prodigal son was more than mere jewelry. As stated previously, the gesture meant that the son's authority and former position were being restored to him.

The incident related in Luke 16:19–31 was not meant to demonstrate that sinners burn eternally in the fires of hell. It is a parable and did not actually or literally happen; however Jesus used the parable to illustrate His point: that He is an advocate for the poor and individuals in possession of material wealth should invest their riches in helping the poor *while they are living.*

Review Questions

1. What three areas are involved with wearing a wedding ring?
2. Fill in the blank: "Gods ideal for this chosen people transcends everything _____ _____."

Chapter 8

Ethical Issues Involved in Wearing the Wedding Band

Ethics has to do with our conduct with a view to duty, morality, and judgment with consideration of future consequences or rewards. There are ethical issues involved in the wearing of wedding bands by SDA and other Christians. Some are herein listed:

1. It is offensive to many believers and violates the principle of **LOVE**. See Romans 13:8–10.
2. It violates the Bible principle of **MODESTY**. See 1 Timothy 2:9 and 1 Peter 3:3, 5.
3. It causes a moral morass, which leads to antinomianism[19] and/or a double standard. It violates the principle against the

---

[19]The belief that one holds that under the gospel dispensation of grace the moral law is of no use or obligation because faith alone is necessary to salvation.

Ethical Issues Involved in Wearing the Wedding Band

wearing of jewelry. It violates the principle of **HONESTY**. See 1 Corinthians 15:33.
4. It is in opposition of explicit prohibitions in the Bible against the wearing of jewelry. The principle of **OBEDIENCE** to God is violated.
5. It exploits the Bible's silence on its use as a symbol to solemnize a wedding, thus doing away with God's "the laying on of hands." Principle: **STEALING**. See Genesis 48:14, Acts 13:3, 8:13, Hebrews 2:2
6. It causes subjects of God to exhibit the trappings or trademarks of another god. Principle: **IDOLATRY**. See Exodus 20.
7. It misleads others and causes them to stumble because of their influence, violating the principle of **LOVE FOR/TO THY NEIGHBOR**. See Galatians 5:22 and 1 Corinthians 13:13.

Review Questions

1. Fill in the blanks: "Ethics has to do with our _____ with a view to _____, _____and _____ with consideration of future _____ or _____."
2. What are the seven ethical issues involved with wearing the wedding ring?

Chapter 9

What are the Options Available?

It appears as though the Seventh-day Adventists and many other church leaders in conservative denominations have opted for a type of graded absolutism (see glossary) in that since they cannot control the situation, they are leaving it to the individual's personal concept of Christian ethics. Consequently, many either through blindly and tenaciously holding onto the superstitious attraction of the wedding ring or carelessly depending upon the "culture" argument, are making the wrong choice. Ministers who close their minds against enlightenment on this issue, who encourage the use of and who try to discount the plain evidence against this form of idolatry (the wedding ring), are playing a deadly game of self-deception and deceiving the people also. God will judge in this matter ... we can be sure. The

What are the Options Available?

> *Do not worry about what people say or think. You owe them nothing. You owe God everything.*

writer's task is only to inform. Each person must decide for himself!

Because things are in such a "big mess," this writer would reluctantly recommend the previously mentioned ethical position with the following suggestions:

1. Seek more knowledge on the subject with an open mind. Pray and ask God to help you to accept what may be new and different to how you formerly thought about jewelry. Also think about God's principles which never change, even though society is continually evolving its concept of what is right or wrong.

2. Cultivate fundamental FAITH. Do not worry about what people say or think. You owe them nothing. You owe God everything.
3. If you put God first in your life, a change in your lifestyle and thinking will result.

Review Questions

1. What are three approaches one could take in the matter of jewelry and wedding ring in the Christian Church?

   a.

   b.

   c.

Appendix A

Note 1: "Confiding then in the power of Christianity to resist the infection of evil and to transmute the very instruments and appendages of demon worship to an evangelical use, we are told by Eusebius that Constantine, in order to recommend the religion to the heathen, transferred into it the outward ornaments to which they had been accustomed to in their own ... The use of temples, and these dedicated to particular saints, and ornamented on occasions with branches of trees, incense lamps, candles; votive offerings on recovery from illness, holy processions, blessings on the field, sacerdotal vestments, THE RING IN MARRIAGE, turning to the east, images at a later date, perhaps the ecclesiastical chant, ALL ARE OF PAGAN ORIGIN, and sanctified by their adoption into the church."
—J. H. Cardinal Newman, *An Essay on Development of Christian Doctrine,* pp. 272, 273.

Note: This statement comes from the Roman Catholic Church.

Note 2: "Your Majesty," one of the Puritans said to the King, "We be a simple people and we wish to worship our Lord in a simple manner. *We wish to be relieved of the superstitions of the Church. We do not want to be required to use the Ring in the marriage ceremony.* We do not want to be made to bow down when repeating the name of Jesus."

—McCarthy, James R., *Rings Through the Ages* (New York: Harper & Brothers, 1945), p. 2.

Note: This statement was made to King James of Scotland and England by a group of Puritans about AD 1603.

Note 3: "A circle, known as a finger-ring, has been an object of ornament and use for thousands of years. Indeed, the time when it was first fashioned and worn is so far in the past that it alone shines there; *all round is ashes and darkness*. This is undoubtedly true. The author might have gone on to say that hovering over the ashes and darkness there is the mist of superstition ... FOR SUPERSTITION is often the beginning of things; of fears, sometimes of sentiment, often of habit. It is at the beginning of objects of wear and adornment--and the ring is one of them. And because superstition so dominates the ring it is given prior consideration in this book."

—McCarthy, James R., *Rings Through the Ages* (New York: Harper & Brothers, 1945), p. 2.

Note 4: "The ring (wedding or betrothal) was simply a symbol of the bridegroom's (or his family's) purchasing power." Claudia De Lys says in *How the World Weds* that the caveman's band around the wrists and ankles of his mate were of braided rushes or grasses; that in time only the wrists were tied with these bands; and that finally the rush ring was woven around the finger. Paul Berdanier in *How It Began* informs us that "our earliest ancestors thought a rope tied around part of the body would keep the soul from escaping. When a man captured his mate, he tied cords around her waist, wrists and ankles to make obedience of the wearer to a higher power."

—McCarthy, James R., *Rings Through the Ages* (New York: Harper & Brothers, 1945), pp. 152, 154.

"Women have always—or rather, have in modern times—resented the claim that a bridal ring meant possession or subjection. Of course the claim is historically authentic."
—McCarthy, James R., *Rings Through the Ages* (New York: Harper & Brothers, 1945), p. 162.

"The ring was used as a symbol for the marriage by purchase, which was doubtless customary among all races."
— "Ring," in *The Jewish Encyclopedia* (New York: Funk and Wagnalls, 1906), p. 428.

Appendix B

Excerpts from: Jewelry, Yesterday & Today[20]

by R. R. Beitz
Former Vice President, General Conference of Seventh-day Adventists

Note 1: Early Christians frowned upon the ring as a worldly adornment. "We read that the wealthy Christians in the time of the apostles wore gold rings but that the anti-Nicene and post-Nicene fathers alike found it necessary to declare against prodigality of Christians who wore rings; not of gold but of bronze. There is no doubt, however, that in the days of Mary and Joseph rings were

---

[20]Beitz, R. R. Review and Herald Publishing Association, Part 3 of a series on church standards, April 21, 1966.

worn; though neither the Bible or the Talmud speaks of the ring as symbolic of marriage."
—McCarthy, James R., *Rings Through the Ages* (New York: Harper & Brothers, 1945), p. 118.

Note 2: "Sapphires were particularly powerful and believed to act as an antidote to poison, and to protect the chastity of their wearers. They were also believed to safeguard their wearer from poverty, wrongful arrest, betrayal, and conviction, and to preserve his reputation from malicious attack. Cardinals themselves wore a sapphire in their finger-rings, for it was commonly supposed to have been the stone upon which God gave the Law to Moses."[21]

Note 3:

A Change in Attitude
Within the past few decades there has been a change in attitude on the part of some. More and more members are wearing wedding rings, especially younger couples. Two wars partly explain this. One author points out that "with the coming of the war, home never seemed so precious to the young man. The soldier clung poignantly to home and wife and all that his marriage meant. Bridegrooms began insisting on a double-ring ceremony. A ring was about all of home they could carry off to war. The young war bride demanded that her soldier husband have some appropriate reminder of his marital status while traveling around the globe. By the end of 1944, the proportion of double-ring ceremonies was something like 95 per cent of the total"[22]

Most of the young women working in factories and offices, surrounded by other people, wanted to identify by the wearing of the wedding ring that they were married. They felt that this was a necessity and saved them from embarrassments. Within recent years it now appears that in the minds of many, a wedding ring is no longer an ornament, but a cultural necessity here in America as in Europe. *But the fact remains that the greatest protection for*

---

[21]Binder, Pearl. *Muffs and Morals* (London: G. G. Harp, 1953).
[22]McCarthy, James R., *Rings Through the Ages* (New York: Harper & Brothers, 1945), p. 182.

any woman is not the ring, but her own positive Christian experience, which will be manifested in Christ-likeness of character, in words and deeds. It is that fact that ever provided the basis for our denominational position regarding the wedding ring.

Besides, there is always the danger that we will go beyond the simple wedding ring and start other jewelry, which is purely ornamental and decorative. The culture may demand rings, necklaces, earrings, and other jewelry, for the sake of adornment. But the culture of our land and times is not a safe guide for the Christian. If we accept every cultural change we can no longer be God's singular people. Certainly the church has had, and still has, a very sensible approach in the matter of wearing jewelry. We have tried to emulate the Master and give attention to the spiritual. To seek first the kingdom of God should be the motto of every child of God.

The Wedding Ring's Seamy Side
Rings in general, and wedding rings in particular, have symbolized different things down through the centuries. Nor are wedding rings necessarily a proof of marriage. We are told that wedding rings are manufactured at the rate of 850,000 a month. One leading magazine, commenting on this fact, declares: "If all these rings were to be used by brides in genuine weddings, every adult American female would have a ring finger decorated like the neck of an Ubangi and would have to contract (shocking as it may seem) a new marriage every five years. Obviously most of the rings are used merely for immoral purposes. The big ten cent stores do a remarkable business in cheap wedding rings selling for 6 or 7 million dollars a year to both occasional and steady customers."[23] This is the other side, the seamy side, of the matter of wedding rings. [The foregoing statement, though "dated" by more than forty years, is still relevant today.]

Through the centuries there have been cultural changes, and many of these have been weird and fantastic. THE CHURCH NEVER COULD ACCEPT THE PREMISE THAT SHE MUST FIT INTO ANY AND ALL CULTURAL PATTERNS.

---
[23]Wallace, Robert, "More Rings than Brides," *Life Magazine*, June 18, 1951.

ALTHOUGH "FASHION IS A MISTRESS THAT RULES WITH AN IRON HAND,"[24] HER "IRON HAND" SHOULD NOT RULE AND DICTATE TO THE CHURCH.

Customs Change; Principles Remain
All of this points out the fact that jewelry does change its symbolism from century to century, and many times assumes bizarre, ridiculous, absurd, and even evil connotations.

Christians should maintain a steady course, and not assume the characteristics of the chameleon. They should be giving more attention to the inner adornment than the outward. We should appreciate a church that has the courage to say "No!" to the world with its ever-changing fashions.

I believe our young people have more respect for a church that strives to live in harmony with New Testament standards. In most churches today there are few that still live as "strangers and pilgrims on earth." A worlding would no longer feel strange in most popular churches [including the Adventist church]. He would hardly see any difference between those professing Christianity and those who don't. When the church no longer presents a challenge for heroic Christian living, we may be sure that she is no longer following the steps of Jesus.

An anonymous clergyman wrote an article entitled "Why I Quit the Ministry." He is one of the many who have resigned from the ministry within recent years. Why did he resign? He said he resigned because he could not find any desire in the hearts of the congregation to take their religion seriously. Speaking about church standards, he said, "Why, we hadn't even the membership standards of a Kiwanis Club."[25] He made the further observation that he would refuse to waste his life in directing this mutual admiration society.

Recently there came a book from the press entitled *Neurotics in the Church*. The author, Robert St. Clair, says, "Our distorted culture makes a fetish of such idols as perfection of beauty and

---

[24]White, Ellen G., *Education* (Mountain View, CA: Pacific Press Publishing Association, 1903), p. 246.
[25]*Saturday Evening Post*, November 17, 1962, p. 36.

talent, and it worships status, superiority of prestige and lofty heights of money power. WHEN THE CHURCH ADAPTS TO A RIGHTEOUS-COATED PAGANISM, THE LINE BETWEEN THE CHURCH AND THE WORLD BECOMES INCREASINGLY HAZY."[26]

---

[26]St. Clair, Robert J., *Neurotics in the Church* (Westwood, NJ: Revell, 1963), p. 20.

Epilogue

The late Elder C. D. Brooks, former speaker for the Breath of Life Telecast, said to me when he perused my book, "God sends truth, not to hurt or embarrass; but to build up and strengthen." Therefore, the author of *Jewelry in God's Church, Why?* does not propose to defend against every rebuttal or objection offered to the information presented here. The historical facts are extant for everyone to read and accept or reject. My prayer is that you are blessed as you read.

—*Pastor Charles E. Creech, Author*

Glossary

Adornment: Decoration which attempts to add beauty.

Amulet: A "good luck" charm or a talisman usually carried on the person.

Conference: An administrative district composed of a number of churches; similar to a diocese or the organizational structure in the Methodist church.

Culture: The development of the mind or body by education, training or socialization.

Defacto (Latin): Actually existing, whether lawful or not.

Frit: Mixture of sand and fluxes or metals which melt at relative low temperatures.

General Conference: The administrative and corporate world headquarters of the Seventh-day Adventist Church, having jurisdiction over all other administrative components of the organization.

Graded Absolutism: An ethical option that attempts to both preserve moral absolutes and yet provide a realistic approach to genuine moral conflicts.

Glossary

Leavening Process: A term used to indicate the inception and growth of compromise in the church. Leaven is actually bacteria which produces carbon dioxide which makes dough rise. Characteristically it grows quickly and spreads rapidly and lives long under ideal conditions.

Mithraism: A cultish, mystery religion involving sacrifices, blood, evil, and darkness.

Ornamentation: The addition of decorations or embellishment.

Postum®: A natural, caffeine-free beverage made from toasted grain that tastes much like coffee.

Quartz Faience: Glazed quartz or glazed earthenware.

Sabbath: The seventh day of the week (Genesis 2:2, 3 and Exodus 20:9–11), the worship day of Seventh-day Adventists and other Sabbath keepers.

Sumptuary: Having to do with the spending of money; regulating expenses especially to control extravagance or waste.

Bibliography

Abrahams, Israel. *Jewish Life in the Middle Ages.* London: The MacMillan Company, 1896.

Aldred, Cyril. *Ancient Jewelry.* New York: Ballantine Books, 1978.

Battke, H. *Geschichte des Ringes.* Baden-Baden: The British Museum, 1953.

Beitz, R. R. Part 3, series on church standards. Washington, DC: Review and Herald Publishing Association, 1966.

Binder, Pearl. *Muffs and Morals.* London: G. G. Harp, 1953.

Book of the Dead, The. Karl Richard Lepsius, trans. https://1ref.us/18x (accessed May 18, 2020).

Budge, E. A. Wallis. *Amulets and Superstitions*, 2nd edition. New York: Dover Publications, 2011.

Dalton, Ormond M. *Catalogue of Early Christian Antiquities in the British Museum.* London: Published by the order of the Trustees, 1901. https://1ref.us/18y (accessed May 19, 2020).

Franks Bequest. Catalogue of the Finger Rings, Early Christian, Byzantine, Teutonic, Mediaeval and Later. London: Printed by the order of the Trustees, 1912. https://1ref.us/18z (accessed May 19, 2020).

Jewish Encyclopedia, The. New York: Funk and Wagnalls, 1906.

Bibliography

King, C. W. *Antique Gems and Rings,* 2 Vols. London: Bell and Daldy, 1866. https://1ref.us/190 (accessed May 19, 2020).

Marshall, F. H. *Catalogue of the Finger Rings.* London: British Museum, 1907, 1968. https://1ref.us/191 (accessed May 19, 2020).

McCarthy, James R. *Rings Through the Ages.* New York: Harper & Brothers, 1945.

Newman, John Henry Cardinal. *An Essay on Development of Christian Doctrine.* Notre Dame, IN: University of Notre Dame Press, 1994.

St. Clair, Robert J. *Neurotics in the Church.* Westwood, NJ: Revell, 1963.

Wallace, Robert. "More Rings than Brides." *Life Magazine,* June 18, 1951.

White, Ellen G. *Education.* Mountain View, CA: Pacific Press Publishing Association, 1903.

White, Ellen G. *SDA Bible Commentary, Vol. 2—EGW Comments.* Washington, DC: Review and Herald Publishing Association, 1953.

White, Ellen G. *Testimonies for the Church, Vol. 4.* Mountain View, CA: Pacific Press Publishing Association, 1881.

White, Ellen G. *Testimonies to Ministers and Gospel Workers.* Mountain View, CA: Pacific Press Publishing Association, 1923.

About the Author

Charles E. Creech is a retired pastor from the Northeastern Conference of Seventh-day Adventists. He is a graduate of Oakwood University ('76) with a BA in theology and business administration and of Andrews University Theological Seminary in Berrien Springs, Michigan, MA in ministry ('91).

A fourth generation SDA, he has served the church for nearly forty-five years as a literature evangelist, associate publishing secretary, Adventist Book Center manager, and pastor, respectively. He is a certified alcohol and substance abuse counselor ('96 to present). Pastor Creech is the author of the requirements for the honor in model boats found in the *Adventist Youth Honors Handbook*.

Historical and Contemporary Perspectives is his publication for addressing important historical and contemporary issues confronting large numbers of people generally and Seventh-day Adventists specifically. It is a teaching tool in his local church and the community of Christian believers throughout the world.

TEACH Services, Inc.
P U B L I S H I N G

We invite you to view the complete
selection of titles we publish at:
www.TEACHServices.com

We encourage you to write us
with your thoughts about this,
or any other book we publish at:
info@TEACHServices.com

TEACH Services' titles may be purchased in
bulk quantities for educational, fund-raising,
business, or promotional use.
bulksales@TEACHServices.com

Finally, if you are interested in seeing
your own book in print, please contact us at:
publishing@TEACHServices.com

We are happy to review your manuscript at no charge.

www.ingramcontent.com/pod-product-compliance
Lightning Source LLC
Chambersburg PA
CBHW070545170426
43200CB00011B/2568